2007

www.bloomingtwigbooks.com

Other Books by Cynthia Blomquist Gustavson

Poetry

Sick-A-War Tree

The Battle Within

I Don't Write Love Poems

Scents of Place

Ruach

Poetry Therapy

In-Versing Your Life: A Poetry Workbook
For Self-Discovery and Healing

Fe-vers: Feeling Verses for Children

Fe-vers: Feeling Verses for Teens

Re-Versing Your Pain: A Poetry Workbook
For Those Living With Chronic Pain

Con-Versing With God: Poetry For
Pastoral Counseling and Spiritual Direction

Spirituality

Human Spirit, Holy Spirit

Kingdom Words

www.cynthiagustavson.com
www.bloomingtwigbooks.com

RE-VERSING THE NUMBERS

A *Poetry Workbook for Eating Disorders*

Poetry and Text by
Cynthia Blomquist Gustavson, MSW, LCSW, ACSW

NEW YORK

Several poems in this manuscript have previously appeared in <u>Scents of Place: Seasons of the St. Croix Valley</u>, by Cynthia Blomquist Gustavson. Published by Country Messenger Press, Marine on St. Croix, MN, copyright ©1987.

Several poems in this manuscript have previously appeared in <u>Where the Wind Comes From</u>, by Cynthia Blomquist Gustavson. Published by Holden Press, Tulsa, OK, copyright ©2001.

Several poems in this manuscript appear in <u>In-versing Your Life</u>, <u>Ruach</u>, <u>The Battle Within</u>, <u>I Don't Write Love Poems,</u> and <u>Sick-a-War Tree</u>, by Cynthia Blomquist Gustavson. Published by Blooming Twig Books, East Setauket, NY, copyright ©2006.

Other poems in this manuscript have appeared in *Sundays at Four,* Shreveport, LA.

Re-Versing the Numbers copyright ©2006-7 Cynthia Gustavson. Tulsa, Oklahoma.
www.cynthiagustavson.com
First Edition Published 2006 by Blooming Twig Books
3A Detmer Road
East Setauket, NY, 11733.
www.bloomingtwigbooks.com
1-866-389-1482
Catalog #: BT002

Second Blooming Twig Books Printing 2007.

ISBN 978-0-9777736-8-8

Dedicated to the Hilton Head Health Institute
in Hilton Head, South Carolina:

*Where I first used some of these poems to help
lovely people 'Reverse the Numbers'*

CONTENTS

VI. COGNITIVE THERAPY AND SELF-TALK   63

VII. COGNITIVE THERAPY AND COMMUNICATION SKILLS   73

X. HEALTH AND WELLNESS

ABOUT THE AUTHOR

INTRODUCTION

As a psychotherapist I often see clients, with eating disorders, who have been through non-helpful behavioral programs. Behaviorism is only part of the answer. Even cognitive change is affected by feelings, and if those feelings remain hidden, then little can be changed. I feel that poetry, as used in this book, is one of the best ways to reconnect with hidden feelings.

There is a need to address the myriad problems of those suffering with eating disorders, a population that is continuing to grow. Therapists are constantly asking me for user-friendly materials which use the arts. The topics covered in this book are cognitive/behavioral in theory, but are approached from the holistic, artistic side, a "right-brain" approach. This book is designed to be used not only by individual readers, but also by mental health professionals. It can be used with hospitalized patients, or with out-patients, as a preventive measure with people who may be just starting to show signs of binging, purging, or starving, and with those in post-hospitalization programs.

This book addresses issues in an emotional, yet sensitive way, and encourages readers to respond to those issues with their own writing. The workbook is designed with a poem on the left-facing page and a writing exercise about the same subject on the right-facing page. This book is a workbook, and the reader can easily read the poems, respond to them, and then write a poem or journal entry in response. It can then be used as therapeutic material within the therapy session, or group session, or used individually by a reader. Poetry homes in on feelings in a uniquely fast and intense manner.

Poetry therapy has been used for centuries. What's unique about this workbook is that it offers the therapist, who is not trained in poetry therapy, and is not a professional poet or English teacher, the use of this technique. It offers the same to an individual reader who may use this book on his/her own. Poetry helps the reader uncover deep feelings and forgotten memories. The writing techniques allow readers to express themselves in an artistic and deeply emotional way. The topics that are covered in the book are all cognitive/behavioral based subjects, but are looked at through a right-brain approach.

Specifically, the areas covered in the book include: Understanding my body; understanding my relationship to food; understanding my emotions; behavioral change; changing irrational thinking; self-talk; communication skills; family dynamics; interacting with the world; and health and wellness.

After a reader uses the exercises in this book I would hope that he/she would be able to define his/her own motivations for behavior, be able to understand the feelings which underlie behavior, be able to use self-talk and other techniques to change behavior, and then be better able to move on to a healthy life style. I would also hope that this workbook encourages the reader/writer to continue to read and write poetry for pleasure, self-understanding and a lifetime of health.

4

I. UNDERSTANDING MY BODY

WHOSE BODY IS THIS?

My hair is blond, but it's turning brown.
It's always been straight, but now I've found
the ends curl and it's no longer dry.
What's happening to me? I can't deny
there's a layer of fat around my hips
that travels from chest to fingertips.
My rings don't fit. My jeans are tight.
I want my body left alone! All right?!
I didn't ask for my breasts to change -
to look in the mirror and feel so strange.
I don't wanna be sexy. I don't wanna talk.
Lemme be the skinny kid from down the block.

How is My Body Changing?

Are you comfortable in your body? Is it what you expected? Do you recognize yourself? What cultural and behavioral differences come with an adult body? Do boys/girls/men/women look at you differently? Do they expect something different from you? Can you talk about your body changes and expectations with parents or friends?

In the above poem the girl narrator states that she doesn't want to be perceived as sexy. Have you ever felt that way? Did it seem as though one day boys were asking you the answers to math questions, and the next day they were calculating your chest size? How can you handle the way you are perceived by others?

Write a poem about your experiences called *Changing/Rearranging...*

ONLY ONE WAY

There is only one way to clean a bowl,
flour and yeast glued to glass walls.
You soak it overnight, then use your
strong fingers to loosen stuck-on dough.
Do not use a scrubber getting glue in every tiny hole,
leaving the bowl with scratches it does not deserve.
Do not use a cloth, later thrown into the wash.
There is only one way to clean a bowl.
Use your own nimble fingers. Slide along
the glass. Find stuck masses. Loosen lumps
of dough. Let them flow out of control
into a cool stream of running water.

Body Scan

What in the world does cleaning a bowl have to do with a healthy lifestyle? When you clean it, you experience it fully, each slick curve is felt and examined. Now do the same with your own body. It's called a body scan.

Start at the top of your head and feel the curvature of your scalp, the softness of your hair, the bone structure of your face. These are areas with which you are familiar from looking in the mirror. But now scan your whole body. Get to know lengths and widths, joints and bones, muscle mass and fatty deposits. It's okay to know your body. It's yours.

It's important to have an accurate perception of your body. Can you feel only bone? Where and what size are your muscles? When your legs are together do your calf muscles touch? When you flex your arm can you see your muscle? The more ownership you take in your own body, the more pride you will have in keeping it active and healthy.

In the space below write a paragraph about what you discovered.

IMAGE

Thin is in,
except for breasts
and outlined muscles

muscles on long
feminine legs
and arms.

Armed with weights
I lift and lower
as I train.

Trained to be gentle,
I now push body
and mind.

I don't mind, really.
I'd rather be strong
as long

as I remain
feminine, as long
as I remain free

free of what others
want of me, free
to choose.

If I lose choice
I lose it all.
What to choose:

A body, like a model,
thin, spare, would
I starve

to get there?
to stay there?
Why there?

A body, like Dolly Parton,
would I pay a surgeon
to get there?

Pay a surgeon to
thin out my nose,
un-wrinkle my skin?

Why there? Is my hair
the wrong color, my
lips too thin?

Now I'm back to thin
again and again
and again.

Thin is in, except for
lips and breasts
and now the muscle trend.

Thin - is in,
but so is sexy, and
being your own woman.

Body Image

What is your body type? What would you like your body type to be? Why? Is your self image influenced by models, magazine ads, movie stars, rock or country western singers, your parents, your peers? Is the body type you want attainable? Would it be healthy? Is it sustainable? Do you judge others by their body image? Why or why not? What body image is healthy for you? Is it the same or different from media images for people your age? How do you disregard media images of the "ideal body," and concentrate on what is healthy for you?

Draw a picture of yourself on the page below. Don't worry about your drawing ability. Review the previous exercise (body scan) and draw your body as it is now. Answer these questions: Is this a *healthy* body? Is this a *beautiful* body? By what standards am I judging it? Do I need to make any changes in order to insure that my body is healthy?

READY FOR COMBAT

This spring there's a war going on,
and signs, letters, calls, poems, not even new life
bursting from the soil, can turn it off.

I plant seeds, water them well, plan each row
for color and space, place tomatoes in cages
and bind beans to their poles.

In the garage I dig my hands
into a dirty box and find the clipper
sharpened last fall, ready for combat.

Euonymous is first, too full and lush.
Its bush covers my lilies. I snip. I prune. I slash.
I clip. I sculpt. I amputate its invading limbs,

Then boxwood, holly, azalea,
prickly pyrocantha, bridal wreath …
even the graceful, white, bridal wreath.

I cut. I slash. I amputate
any spring growing thing in my way.
There is a war going on.

At War With My Body

What wars are raging in your life? Are you at war with your family? Your doctor? Therapist? With food? With fat? With people who are trying to "control you"? Do you take it out on your own body?

What are the guns, bullets and knives of your war? Are there alternatives to war? What are they?

The word "war" spelled backwards is "raw." Write a poem using those two words.

14

II.   UNDERSTANDING
MY RELATIONSHIP TO FOOD

STRAWBERRIES

High noon found
June-berries hidin'
hot feet diggin' in the coal black dirt
careful not to crush lush red or green unripe.
De-topped and bucket-washed, speckled mounds
are sliced and spiced for white icy treats,
boiled for jam, tapioca'd for pie,
or left cool and damp for eatin'
in the sun, one by one,
with juice-stained fingers
pleadin' to be licked --
and more in the garden
needin' to be picked.

Pleasurable Food Association

The poem tells about the pleasure of picking, eating and preparing fresh strawberries for treats. Close your eyes and see if you can visualize yourself in that patch, smelling the ripe sweetness, tasting the tiny berries on your tongue. Is there one food that brings you pleasure because of its taste, but also because you associate something wonderful with it?

Write a poem with the following lines:

I remember the smell . . .

I remember the color . . .

I remember the texture . . .

I remember the time of year . . .

I remember the place I found it . . .

I remember the feeling it gave me . . .

I remember . . .

COMFORT

I cook potato soup in fall.
I need all its thick starch
to fill darkening nights.

I bake bread when I'm cold.
Its yeast unfolds in my animal brain
and recalls loaf-warm kitchens.

I make popcorn when I'm scared,
its kernels daring to escape
my pot and bowl.

I drink cocoa when I'm rejected,
its warm sweetness protecting
my every need.

I eat oatmeal each morning,
each warm grain warning:
I am ready.

Comfort Food

What food is comforting to you? Something warm? Something your mother or grandmother used to make for you when you were sick? Something with a great aroma, such as bread out of the oven or fresh brewed coffee? We know why food comforts us. It warms or cools us, puts sugar into our brains, calms our stomachs and stirs memories of better times. The problem in our 21st century is that we are living with enormous levels of stress. Our bodies tell us to calm down, slow down, relax, but we don't have the time for that, so we reach for comfort food, and hope it will restore us to a more peaceful demeanor. It alone cannot perform that miracle for us.

How often do you use food for comfort? If you binge, is it comfort foods you reach for? How comforting are these foods if they become part of the binge/purge cycle? What other stress relievers do you use? Which of them is healthiest?

Write a poem about the word "comfort", thinking of as many examples as you can.

COMFORT

Comfort is a flannel quilt on a cool night.

Comfort is . . .

Comfort is . . .

Comfort is . . .

Comfort is . . .

Comfort is . . .

ALTERNATIVES

Jack Sprat could eat no fat
his wife could eat no lean
and so between them both, you know,
they licked the platter clean.

But that, alas, was in years past
when platters just had meat,
but now we have soup and nuts and fruit
and dairy and pasta to eat.

I bet Jack would like peanuts for a snack
and his wife could dine on tofu
that was spiced just right with tamari light
or experience a lentil stew.

There's food of worth from the whole wide earth
which takes little time to prepare,
so if you're a Jack, grab a grocery sack,
and stuff it with no room to spare.

And if you're his wife, take serious your life,
and start eating lean in your diet.
Pick carefully your fruit, your nuts and your soup
and if it's not healthy, don't buy it.

Healthy Alternatives

Since we now have access to foods, recipes and spices from all over the world, healthy, exciting eating has become easier. Try free-range chicken, pita bread, mangoes, papaya, zatar spice. Go to a gourmet or an alternative food store and buy one new item. (You can begin small with a new spice or fruit.) Ask someone in the store how to use it. After you have found one new item that you enjoy, write about the experience.

Write a poem with the title *The New Item on Jack or Mrs. Sprat's Table*.

LOVE FOOD

She knew how to work, came from the old country and never took time to learn to smile, just worked as a waitress in her white apron, taking orders, bringing hot platefuls of meat and potatoes to men working just as hard as she, and one day one asked in his Swedish tongue to marry her and she took enough time to say *yes*, and she asked him, *would you help me run my own restaurant*? and he said *yes*, and took enough time to learn to wash dishes while she cooked and delivered hot platefuls of Swedish meatballs and pancakes and limpa bread to the hungry hardworking immigrants of Chicago.

And they had a boy who died in his daddy's arms as he choked for breath from his suffocating pneumonia. And they had another son, who would not die, she would make sure he would not die, and she fed him in the midst of America's depression, she fed him meatballs and pancakes and limpa and pie. In the depression he ate strawberry meringue pie. He grew up to be a man who expected to be fed pie, and when he felt other's rejection, he didn't seek hugs, he looked for food, and because he knew how to work hard and was successful, he didn't ask for meatballs or limpa, he wanted steak and lobster, topped off with pie. This grown-up child of immigrants, this child of work and few smiles took every opportunity to feed his family well.

〰〰

What Does Food Represent

The prose poem on the left page tells the story of a mother who tried to convey love through food. Think about what you associate with food, especially certain kinds of food. Were you forced to eat foods you did not like? Was food treated as something special, or something you needed in order to survive? Was it given as a reward for good behavior, taken away for bad behavior? Imagine your mother (or other caregiver) cooking dinner. Did you help? What did it smell like? What was it like sitting around the table at mealtime? Was this a time of relaxation or tension?

Write a poem with the title *Memories Served on a Platter...*

THE GIFT OF TOMATOES

The old woman
comes with bags
of fruit, tomatoes
from her garden,
the taste sweet and
almost forgotten.
Unlike store bought,
they leave a pungent
odor in my hand.

A garden gift,
no matter how
often received,
is a lifting of each
round fruit, each
ripe moment, saying,
Take this. Eat.
Make it part of you.

"Make it Part of You"

Clothes you can use and throw away. A house you can live in and leave. Friends can come and go. But the food you eat becomes part of you. That is a unique relationship. The poem suggests that food is a gift, almost sacred, "a lifting of each ripe moment." Do you agree? Is food (and the eating of it) an obligation, a blessing, a gift, a curse, a ritual, a necessity? How would you describe it?

On the page below quickly write six words you think of when you hear the word "food." Then write two more words associated with each of the six words. Write a poem using the associated words and describing your feelings about eating.

III. UNDERSTANDING
MY EMOTIONS

HOW DO I FEEL TODAY?

Is it exasperated, exhausted, pleased, enraged,
optimistic, pessimistic, detached or engaged,
determined, disgusted, bashful or bored,
over-anxious, confident, blissful or ignored,

apologetic, arrogant, agonized, smug,
or pleased and peaceful as a bug on a rug?
Sometimes I feel as if I were demure -
but most of the time, I'm not really sure.

Today I am curious, idiotic, ecstatic,
envious, hysterical, and getting combatic -
so don't you get cold or aggressive or surly,
or make me mad or wake me up early.

Tomorrow I might be meditative, withdrawn,
writing love letters while lying on the lawn.
Whatever I feel . . . it's okay with me.

(And by the way . . . You can disagree!)

Identifying Feelings

If you had asked me as a child to identify all of my feelings, I would have listed *happy, sad, mad* and *neutral.* But I have since learned how complex feelings really are.

Look at the above poem and see how many of those feelings you have felt in the last week. Identifying feelings is the first step in dealing with them. Try not to judge your feelings. All feelings are human and they have a purpose. They act as red flags to tell us when something is right in our life, or something is unfinished, or not right and needs to be worked on.

Write a poem called *I Feel This Minute*, and write it as you feel it.

If you feel small, write small, if you feel tall, write it out in tall letters.

Are you feeling d e t a c h e d ? How about idiotic ?

ALL I WANT . . .

All I want to do is

 (hide)

All I want to do is   rrrrrrrrrrr uuuuuuuuuuu nnnnnnnnnnnnnnn !!!!!!!!

ALL I WANT TO DO IS

                    D
                       R
                          O
                             P

                                      I
                                         N
                                            T
                                         O

                          A

            H
          O   L
            E

                                          ALL I WANT TO DO IS

                                     YELL!

                                        〰

Expressing Feelings

What's keeping you from yelling, from running, from hiding? Is there ever an appropriate time for those things? What do you do with your feelings? Do you always tell everyone what you feel? Do you always keep your feelings to yourself? Do you deny that you even have feelings? What would you like to express to someone right now? Is anyone listening?

Write a poem in the form of a letter to someone who doesn't understand your feelings. It could also be written to yourself. In it tell him/her/you what you really want.

Dear ____

i wanna feel

better than i feel
anything is better than i feel

for ma its strong coffee
cup after cup and
no one tells her to stop
even when her legs bounce
and she can't sleep

and dad comes home to
scotch on cold clear rocks
the only thing to numb
his anger and rest
his spinning eyes

i need a little help
from a bottle or a pill
i cry *it's to find normal*
not just to get high
but I know

it takes time
for such a long climb

〜〜
〜〜

Mood Alterers

In our world it is common to turn to some sort of mood altering substance for relief of psychological pain. In this poem the mother turns to coffee, which has caffeine, a stimulant. The dad turns to Scotch, alcohol, a depressant. And the narrator in the poem is calling for something to help him/her just feel normal again. We use soda pop, chocolate, tea, prescribed drugs, illegal drugs, alcohol, cigarettes and coffee to alter our moods. Could binging and purging be considered another mood altering behavior? What are the consequences of any of these behaviors? Are some worse than others? Which affect your health? What are healthy ways of getting your body to feel normal when you are upset, sad, bored, frustrated etc? Why is the pronoun "I" not capitalized in this poem? What kind of self-esteem does this person have?

Write a poem using the capital letter "I" and list some natural, healthy ways in which you can lift your mood.

I ...

34

I USED TO BE

I used to be a straight, narrow creek, cold and blue, bursting into white ruffles as I sailed over rocks, logs and dams. I sang as I skipped, and never stopped long enough to learn the names of fish or flowers who depended on my fast, running water. I got where I was going with no interference.

But now I meander, slow my body enough to form pools which warm in summer sunlight. I find I sing more duets than solos now, and the water I share with others is deeper, thicker, slower, warmer. I know different kinds of trout, various colors of aster, and I am now concerned about my path: where I am going, what I have to climb over, is it wide or narrow, will I survive it, and who do I bring along with me.

I Used to Be... But Now I Am...

Try this exercise developed by Kenneth Koch.

Think of some object in nature that is a metaphor for the person you used to be. Then compare it with some other object in nature that describes you as you are today. What is good about each of these images? What is problematic about them? Which feels better?

After you have written, *I used to be . . . but now I am . . . ,*
think about writing, *I am . . . but I will be . . .*

OFF AUTO-PILOT

Keep singin' Harry Belafonte in my head.
Day O, day O, Come da night,
and I wanna go home,
go home in my new Daiwoo (silent W), day oo, day oo,
my new car, come all the way from Korea,
come to Oklahoma,

come to where a dry, cool front
heading down from northern plains rear-ends
the saturated remains of Gulf of Mexico steam,
dents and twists it into winds that
might send a new car flyin'.
Day oo, day oo, come da day and I wanna go home.

Cool air sweeps out of northern plains
lookin' for sizzle, for movement, for entanglement.
Can't go back north. Head my Daiwoo, day oo, day oo, south, til it drips
with perspiration, come Saturday night and I can't find my way home.

Monday I keep singin' Belafonte in my head,
this head twistin' from the north,
stormin' from the south, lookin' for a home to go to,
a place to park my Daiwoo,
day oo, day oo, come da night, and I wanna be home.

Not This, But What?

Do you ever feel bad, but you just can't say why? Do you feel like going anywhere but where you are? Then when you get there you still don't know what you want? What direction are you headed? Is your head "twistin' from the north, stormin' from the south"? Are there floods from the east and drought from the west?

How do you determine what direction to go, and where to stop? Are people asking you to choose a major, a profession, a spouse, a steady boy/girl friend, and you aren't ready to settle down yet? Are you being told what to do and to believe, and you feel you need time to evaluate it all? Start by listening to your feelings. When you feel agitated, stop and figure out what is causing it. When you feel at peace, stop and figure out what is right.

Use this space to journal about what you learn in the process.

IV.   BEHAVIORAL CHANGE

BEFORE THE FALL

Leaves have not changed enough to notice,
haven't yet stored away summer's green.

Today this maple-shape returns as I squeeze
its supple body. Red trims only the rim.

Some outer tips have blackened, but not yet
crisped enough to crumble into dust.

The brush of shorter days will paint them rust
and orange, but change begins at the edges.

41

Signs

What are the signs that you need to make changes in your life? A leaf begins to blacken at the edges. What are your edges showing you? Are you always tired? Do you spend too much time and energy thinking about your weight? Has a doctor warned you about your health? Are people who love you concerned?

On the page below draw a caution sign and write a poem in it about what you see.

THEIR WAY

I did it my way. sung by Frank Sinatra

Let me be frank. I may be ready,
but I didn't get where I am
by doing it my way.

I did it her way, his way, their way,
sometimes no way at all,
but never my way.

My highway never passed by rows of roses,
no sidewalk stretches
to ease my way.

It's been chasing someone else's dog
through chiggared grass
and stepping

on a forgotten arrowhead pointing
to a path which winds its way
into my words.

Whose Way?

Does it seem as though everything you do is because of someone else's rule, someone else's idea of what should be done? If you misbehave, you are punished. If you won't eat, or you purge, or exercise too much, something is taken away. Do you long for the time when you can make your own choices? How can you feel like your own person even when you aren't calling the shots?

What do the last few lines of the poem mean? Does the narrator mean to say that she found herself even in the out-of-control world she lived in? How can you put your stamp on the world in which you live, whether that world is limited or fully free? Think about one situation when you followed orders, but somehow you made it your own.

Write about it in a poem called *The Highway to My Way...*

CHANGE

Ugly worm spin
      as you crawl,
            soon you'll fly with crocheted shawl.

Grasp the sunset
      butterfly-weed,
            your orange will milk to silken seed.

Cumulus cloud
      white, warm,
            accumulate gray laden storm.

Weathervane cock
      whose spin we trust,
            will the winds still shift when
                    slowed
               by
            rust?

What Keeps Us From Changing?

Caterpillars turn into butterflies, flowers into seed, without thinking. White fluffy clouds become storm clouds, without thinking. What is it that keeps you from changing unhealthy behavior? What about this behavior is still serving your purposes?

In the poem it is irrational (or poetic) thinking that says the winds will not shift if we can't measure the shift with our weathervane. What is it about your own thinking that is at times irrational?

Write a poem titled *Shifting Winds.*

WHAT I MISS

The unexpected car driving in
The friendly knock at the door
The hustling away of cards and comics
The bringing out of hidden cookies
A reason for a picked up parlor
A reason for a smooth quilted bed
A surprise in the form of a person
Whether Grandma or the preacher
Cousins looking for hand-me-downs
Neighbors selling magazines
Stinky 'ol Lil looking for a meal
Or friends playing on the lawn.
These treasures out of reach
Are what I miss from moving on.

What I Miss From Moving On

When you make changes in your life, there will be losses as well as gains. If you change your eating or exercise habits what will you lose? What will you gain? If you take control of your life, what will you lose, and what will you gain?

In your mind, if the gains (advantages) outweigh the losses, change is more likely to occur.

Write a poem called *What I Miss (or Will Miss) From Moving On...*

V.   COGNITIVE THERAPY:

CHANGING IRRATIONAL THINKING

SOLID GROUND
Life ain't been no crystal stair. Langston Hughes

They try to make it into a stair,
crystal or no,
tell us we're moving up,
we're on the way, a step ahead,
up another rung,
until we reach a plateau
and where do we go
from there?

I say
we don't need to climb a ladder,
or get high enough to fall,
all we need to do is walk
together on this
flat-on-the-ground circle
stepping around
stones, entering
doorways.

Reframing Behavior

Do you sometimes feel as though you are a failure or that you haven't risen on that success ladder as high as you had expected? Or maybe you have fallen off the ladder?

Take a look at your life and realize that it has brought you to this moment, this page, this thought. You have not fallen. You have learned from all your human mistakes and have arrived here with a new understanding of who you are. The motion is circular, not vertical. You may be learning things about yourself that you knew as a young child, and then forgot, such as how to listen carefully to your body, when it's hungry, and when it's not. Life seemed simpler then. Is there a way to get to that place again, to get rid of guilt, blame, and messages in your head that tell you to succeed at all costs?

Write a poem in the shape of a circle as you write about rediscovering your real self.

MARKED

Did you know
they hanged girls
who had moles,

thought it
marked them
as a witch

in Salem, Massachusetts
three hundred
years ago?

And if you said,
*I didn't ask
for moles,*

they still believed
you were marked
as evil.

People with moles
were scary, different,
witches,

and no matter
what you'd wish,
only decades of time

would change
their minds.
Moles don't

go away, don't
fade like freckles.
They mark you.

〰〰

Judging Others and Being Judged

Do people judge you by something for which you have little or no control? Do you judge others by their skin color, height, weight, their beauty or lack of it, their ability (coordination, intelligence, etc.), their age, gender, culture or family?

Sometimes we judge others, or are judged, by something that happened years ago. What does it feel like to be "marked"? Do you feel as if a label has been assigned to you and you cannot change from that stereotype? How would others describe you? Would that description be accurate or complete? Is it a label that you like or dislike? What can you do about it?

Write your feelings in a free verse poem called *If I Could Erase the Mark...*

NAMES

The Asplundh tree man,
sinewy, with bark-tanned face,
calls me Ma'am.

Doesn't know I'm half Swede,
same as Mr. Asplundh,
doesn't know my name.

He asks me to sign
to clear cut my trees which
dare hang over Swepco wires.

I won't sign,
make him show me the limbs
he is required to cut.

I listen all day to buzzing
and watch the trees,
listen for the whine of the wind,

then head my wheelbarrow
for piles of broad limbs
just right for my fireplace.

He says, *This is junk,*
can't burn pine,
don't waste your time.

I load a white log and say,
This is river birch.
He shrugs his shoulders.

I pick up poplar, oak,
more river birch,
and a little pine won't hurt.

He thinks they are the same,
trees, just trees,
to cut out of the way,

like cancer
or a poison ivy vine
that chokes out life.

His nametag says Mr. Brown,
but he does not know me,
and he does not know the trees,

and he does not know Mr. Asplundh,
the Swede from Chicago
who called tree limbs "quist,"

and he does not know
that in Mr. Asplundh's tongue
my name* means "blooming limb"

*Blomquist

All or Nothing Thinking

This tree trimmer used "all or nothing" thinking. He categorized all trees as the same, something that needed to be cut out of the way of his electric lines. Are you guilty of the kind of thinking that sees everything in terms of black and white and sees no gray areas? Are people fat or skinny? Is everything either right or wrong? Are all women angels or temptresses? Are all men worthless or wonderful? Is the way you think the only way to think? Is everyone else wrong? If we think in terms of black and white, we not only miss the gray areas, we also miss the entire crayon box of 64 colors.

All or nothing thinking contributes to the idea that "I need to look like a model, or no one will like me," or " I have to get straight A's or I'll never be successful in life." If we tell ourselves there is no in-between, we limit ourselves and lose hope.

Take a box of crayons or colored pencils and draw a picture of your family or friends in all their varied sizes. You may want to write a poem after that called *I Dream in Color.*

ALL THAT'S LEFT

I once lived
in a hundred
year old house

        where creaking walls
        conjured dreams
        of dead farmers

who starved
growing corn
on its sand hill

        but stayed around
        to see how it all
        turned out.

The hundred acres are
now carved into fives,
houses peeking

        through pines
        that thrive
        on hills of sand.

The ghost farmers
disappeared when
cedar-sided mansions

        dwarfed the old house,
        and bluestem prairie
        became lawn,

and the pines I planted
forty years ago are
all that's left of wild.

        The pines
        and subdivisions
        thrive on

        hills of sand,
        but I need
        more.

Wants and Needs

The poem says, "But I need more." What do you need? What do you want? Are they the same? Do you sometimes convince yourself that what you want is what you need? Can some of your wants or needs be put off until a future time? Do you want or need adventure, love, support, education, fun, peace, freedom?

Under the column "Want" list those things you want, but are not essential. Under "Need" list those things that you need. Think hard about this. What are your dreams? Do you want, or need, those things you dream about? Are there forgotten dreams or goals that you might recover?

Write about what you discover and call it *But I Need More.*

WANT	NEED

THIEVES

Blasted pinfish
steals shrimp-bait
meant for flounder
then pricks his pins
into my flesh as
I set him free --

It's Sunday on the dock
and I don't need his trouble.

I walk the beach
but receive no gift.
The empty shell
houses a hermit crab
who stole it first and
challenges me to a dual.

Thieves they are, refusing
to respect my ownership

of empty shell and shrimp,
of fish and ocean swell
and all the sands that
tumble and fall and shift
and scratch and finally catch
in my tight leather shoe.

Control

This poem talks about control. What do, and do you not, have control over? Do you need to have (or even should have) control over everything in your environment? How about your body? What do you have control over? What is the place of heredity in body build? How about in other aspects of your life? Do you feel as though you are always following someone else's orders or priorities? Is it age related, sex related, education related? Is there such a thing as partial control, a choice between choices?

Answer these questions in the form of an acrostic poem. The letters from the word "control" are listed vertically on the page. Write your seven line poem beginning each line with a word which begins with the given letter. If you'd like a less controlled poem, write a free verse poem beginning with the word "blasted."

C...

O...

N...

T...

R...

O...

L...

THE DREAM
This is the way the world ends, not with a bang, but a whimper.   T.S. Elliott

I was at
the almost peace
of no breath at all

in my sleep (finally fallen asleep)
when there was no air
everywhere fading dark, quiet

then:
        Get used to this
the dream said

I felt no fear, just
the peace of giving up
I did not try to awaken

and staying there
I did not shout
(no breath to shout)

until on the edge,
a flickering, so weak
I should not have caught the light

with heavy squinted eyes
slowly, lowly,
I faced it.

I had been at
the almost peace of no breath at all
and I did not fall into it
        follow
                follow
    fall out
                        fall in

did not utter the final

                    (whimper)

Suicide

When backed into a corner sometimes suicide seems the only way out. But suicide is deadly not only to the one who dies, but to the whole world. "This is the way the world ends," says Elliott. Why did this person choose to turn to the light instead of accepting death? Is death peace? Is it really an answer to anything?

Think of one person you could turn to when you get to the point of feeling "the almost peace of no breath at all." Make yourself a promise to call that person before trying to hurt yourself.

List below your 10 best reasons to keep on living, even though life may be difficult. Keep this list in your wallet or somewhere near so you can refer to it whenever you need that extra motivation to keep trying.

1.

2.

3.

4.

5.

6.

7.

8.

9.

10.

VI.   COGNITIVE THERAPY:

SELF-TALK

HUNGRY

My stomach isn't growling but I really need to eat
because I'm right now staring at a wonderful treat -

a brownie concoction covered with raspberry gel
and I wasn't even hungry until my eyes beheld

this heavenly delight which makes me salivate -
I wasn't even hungry until I saw this wondrous plate

but I'm sure hungry now even though my belt is tight,
so excuse me as I indulge and take a sweet bite.

Internal and External Locus of Control

Do you eat because you are hungry (internal control,) or are you hungry because you see or smell something to eat (external control)? If we listen to our own body signals, then we know if we are really hungry or if we are just being stimulated by sights or scents of food. If you are in a mall shopping, and you walk by the cookie stall and see the huge and wonderfully smelling delectibles that have just come out of the oven, chances are your brain sends a signal to your control center that says, "Stop. Get out your money. I want one of those now." We all feel that way at times. The best way to counteract those external stimulants to our hunger is through the use of self talk.

List positive self-talk statements below. Write them into a poem called *I Can Talk Myself into Being Healthy.*

Self Talk:
-- I will be eating in less than an hour.
-- I have already had my lunch so I know I am really not hungry yet, and I am too busy to stop here right now.
-- If I don't stop here now I will be able to eat more at dinnertime.
--
--
--

For some, even the internal locus of control stops working. When you have no appetite, no feeling of hunger, or when the hunger sensation goes away with only the ingestion of very little food, then you must work hard to relearn your own body's signals. This takes time and patience. But self-talk can *help*.

Self Talk:
-- I used to love the taste of bread coming out of the oven. I will remember that .
-- One minute ago my stomach was growling. I'm sure I am still hungry.
--
--
--
--

FORBIDDEN FRUIT

Religious men have more illicit affairs
and buy photos of lusty, busty women, hidden
photos which don't resemble wives or mothers.
Lives which control everything else careen
from edge to edge, balance almost broken,
by these unseen acts which are forbidden.

A belligerent two-year-old hides inside bodies
of these ordered adult men and acts out freedom
as if only black and white crayons exist
knowing nothing of freedom and its box full
of varying shades and colors of chance and choice -
golden friendship, turquoise intimacy missed.

The power of "no" upon righteous souls twists
this prohibition into an opposite demand,
creating deeds which shame the best of men
creating space into which strong men fall
and become lame as they listen to inner voices
struggling and whispering "no," then "yes" again.

That Which is Forbidden

Statistics say that often very religious men have problems with pornography and/or extra-marital affairs. We all know the concept of forbidden fruit. If we can't have it, we want it. The thing that is forbidden, or unattainable, takes on larger than life dimensions because of our own inner struggle to deny it.

If your struggle is attaining a body shape that others tell you is unhealthy, how can you deal with that dilemma? If you have a problem with bulimia, and you desire more food than is healthy for you, or you use food as a comfort, which in turn becomes a problem, how do you deal with that psychologically? Is there a middle ground, something between forbidden and good-for-me? What kind of positive self-talk would be appropriate to respond to this problem?

List several self-talk statements below, then choose one and write it into a poem.

<u>For example:</u>
I choose to be healthy, this day, for me.
It's not that I can't have it, it's that I choose to have something better.

JUMPER

When does a squirrel know
he wants to be a burier of nuts,
a digger of holes, a jumper of boughs?

Where does he learn the physics of place,
the mathematics of triangulation,
the manipulation of space?

Who teaches him the courage to steal a nut,
to trespass a private yard,
to leap across unmeasured gulf?

Who gives him grace to walk a telephone wire,
a tightrope high above familiar ground,
where falling would be fatal?

Does he sleep in his nest, one eye
open to intruders, or does he trust,
and whom does he trust?

Does he hold a dug-up acorn in his paws,
sniff its dirty, dusky shell, and ask,
Is it clean enough to eat?

What We Tell Ourselves

Obviously no squirrel asks, "Is this nut clean enough to eat?" But it's a question we humans ask all the time. That's not the only question we ask ourselves about food. How about, "Am I hungry?" "How many calories does this food have?" "Will it make me fat?" "Is the taste worth the calories?" "Is it healthy for me?"

Some of those statements are healthy and some are not. Some are healthy under some circumstances and unhealthy under others.

List below examples of self-talk which are healthy and unhealthy regarding your eating habits. Then choose one of the phrases and write a poem using the phrase several times.

Healthy Self-Talk	Unhealthy Self-Talk

THE FIVE STAGES OF EXCESSIVE WEIGHT LOSS

Denial
Me? Underweight?
I'm not too thin. Don't you see
this fat under my chin?
You're wrong. You don't have a clue.
Leave me alone.
I'm healthier than you.

Anger
I inherited bad traits:
weak heart, bad knees
and a tendency to gain weight.
It makes me so mad.
I won't let getting fat
become my fate!

Bargaining
Just that one taste of pie.
It's so small. Won't hurt at all.
I'll avoid the elevator,
run up and down the stairs,
and I'll skip my lunch
'cause who cares?

Depression
As I push away cheesecake,
chips (chocolate and potato,)
cinnamon rolls and cookies,
apple bars and fettucine alfredo,
all my deprived longings twist
into an inner tornado.

Acceptance
My neighbor has noticed I walk
a little slower. I've taken some time
to get to know her. I don't weigh myself
until week's end, and I've
come to realize carrots
aren't always a girl's best friend.

Examining Your Own Self-Talk

Elizabeth Kubler-Ross discovered the five stages we all go through when we experience loss. This poem is a play on those five stages. If you think about it, there is loss involved in an eating disorder, loss of health. Self-talk can be a way to heal that loss.

Look at each verse in the poem and listen to the self-talk the speaker is using. Does your self-talk sound like that? Which phrases? What phrases could you substitute for the negative self-talk?

Write your own poem using the five stages.

VII. COGNITIVE THERAPY:
COMMUNICATION SKILLS

WAITING TO BE HEARD

Can I say something now?

Of course. I'm listening. Everyone else says I have good communication skills. Don't know why you have so much trouble talking to me.

I was thinking about how . . .

Don't bring up that psychology stuff about me always hurting your feelings, and you know I always do what's best for you, so don't say I don't care.

I just wanted to share . . .

And don't you dare start in about me preaching again today, because you're right, I won't listen. I don't preach and I don't appreciate your telling me I do, so go ahead now, say what you wanted to say.

She started to cry.

Come on now, it's your turn. How do you expect us to communicate when you won't even try?

Communication

There are many ways in which communication fails. This poem is an example of one person's communication being shut off. Why? What happened here? We call it **defensiveness**. The second person was so caught up in defending his/her own self that he/she could not or would not listen to the other person. Has that ever happened to you, either on the defensive end or on the trying-to-communicate end? Let's call it the **BIG D.** The defensive person needs to consciously use self-talk to counteract the tendency to defend (*I'm okay, I can listen, I can learn something,*) bite their tongue and open their ears and mind to the information given by the other person. They will be so surprised that you actually listened that their accusing language or attitude will lessen and hopefully lead to real understanding.

Which of the following statements are defensive statements and will only lead to a fight or no conversation at all?

1. I want to talk about your eating behavior in front of this counselor because then you can't accuse me of being too pushy.
2. I can't talk to you about anything because you always say I'm just a kid and you're an adult.
3. I'd like to talk about how our family communicates.
4. Every time I try to talk about my feelings you say I complain too much, just like Grandma.

Write a typical conversation between you and someone with whom you have been having trouble communicating. When you have finished writing it, go over the conversation and look for signs of the **BIG D.** Rewrite the conversation so that real communication occurs.

WHEELS

No one looks me in the eye and sees
the wheels rotating in my brain,

wheels that spin sometimes out of control
when I'm invisible, when everyone looks away,

when the wheeling and dealing world
whirls round and round without me.

Instead of saying what I did wrong
won't you ask me what I think

and then in patience wait . . .
sometimes for a long time . . . to hear my answer?

I have something important to say, just as much
as if my words came from some library book.

My wheels need oil to keep them spinning.
Don't you know what happens when wheels rust

and metal screeches in its attempt to brake,
spitting sparks into the dry air of a rotating world?

≈

Being Acknowledged

Do you ever feel invisible? Are you there in body, but you feel as if no one acknowledges your presence, and no one wants to hear your opinion? Is there even one person who hears you, values you, doesn't look away (a family member, grandparent, friend, neighbor, coach, teacher, counselor)? How important is that? How do you feel when your wants and needs are ignored? Is it a different feeling to be able to voice your wants and needs, but not necessarily to get them? In an assertive manner from now on *thank anyone who listens to you*, whether they agree with you or not. Little by little you will find your voice and find that others will listen to you as well.

After a while write about this experience.
Call your writing *Listening to My Voice*.

HAIKU

The Canadian goose
pacing near its road-killed mate
honks at speeding cars

Finding Your Voice

What is likely to happen to this Canadian goose out there honking at traffic? Are they listening? Do they understand the message? How do we get cars (people) to slow down and listen before road kill happens? When and where is the best time to "honk"? What happens if we keep silent? What has happened to you in the past when you tried to "honk" at speeding cars? Is "honking" the same as screaming? What other ways of communicating do we have? What ways are listened to most often?

Write a haiku (3 lines, 17 syllables) beginning:

I open my mouth and

_____

_____

AT THE PLACE OF NO CONVERSATION

She visits weekly
but understands
he does not know her

Her smile remains constant
though there is no
greeting in return

Returning is harder
with each trip
to the nursing home

Home seems so far away
at this place
of no conversation

Conversation here
is a touch
of the hand

Hands stiff
and becoming boney
getting cold

Cold eyes
she meets wide-eyed
with hope

And with hope
she brings this time
a guest

Who would have guessed
what Mack, her dog,
could sense?

Scent alone
does not explain
Mack's nuzzling care

Careful now
he licks the coldness
of this hand

Handles taut skin
rubbing the old man
with warm fur

Furrows lift
from the man's eyes
his lips grope to form words

Wordless too long,
he touches Mack,
Come Back

Body Language

In this poem a woman visits a man in a nursing home even though he doesn't recognize her most of the time, and he has lost his speech. When she brings her pet dog, the man seems to come alive again, and even forms words. A dog cannot talk. The man could not talk, but they communicated. How is that possible? What kind of body language do you use? Do you see others using? Is there a certain facial look on a loved one that frightens you, or makes you feel at peace? How do your family members sit at the table? Stiff or relaxed? Friendly and inviting, or judgmental?

Think about the body language of those around you: the face, neck, hands (fists,) open or closed gestures, legs hanging loosely or tightly crossed, smiles, frowns, posture. Then think about your own. Look in a mirror. Examine photos of your self. Ask others. What is your silent communication telling others?

Then write *My Whispering Body is Shouting*.

VIII. FAMILY DYNAMICS

DIFFERENT WAYS

didn't mean it
really didn't
mean to be late
(the tulip tree
caught my eye -
it popped out pink
since last I was there)
didn't mean to ignore
your instructions
(my wandering ears
could hear cicadas
in the trees
along the path -
worn out grass
not yet spring green)
didn't mean
to wander into
different ways

Family Roles

There are many ways to describe personality types. Each of them acknowledges that we are different. Some of us are organized and do everything in the most efficient manner possible. Some of us take crooked paths to smell the flowers on the way, or maybe because the distractions are more interesting than the main events. Sometimes distinct family roles are developed because they are needed to balance a family. Someone needs to be the responsible one, the clown, the scapegoat. If those roles (and others) become fixed and rigid, arguments appear when individuals try to break out of those stereotypes.

Have you ever tried to "find" yourself in ways others do not recognize? How hard is it to change the image of ourselves that others hold? What role do you play in your family? Are you allowed to play other roles? Do you play several roles? If you are the "strong" one, are you allowed to fall apart sometimes? If you are the "rebel," are you allowed to speak for the family? If you are the "intellectual," are you allowed to get a bad grade? If you are the "sick" one, are you allowed to be well? If you are the "perfect" one, are you allowed to make a mistake? If you have always been the "beautiful" one, are you allowed to get fat, to have pimples, to be plain? If you are female, can you do male things (mow lawn, vigorous sports etc.) or vice versa?

Discuss family roles with others in your family. What did you learn? How rigid are your family's roles? Write about what you learn in a poem called *Wandering into Different Ways.*

YOU WANTED

quiet evenings
in the library
reading books

everything in place
pad and pencil
on the desk

well behaved and
loving children
achievers

playing sonatas
before dinner on
miniature violins

then seated at six
napkin-lapped
at their place

the curly-furred dog
lying quietly
at your feet

♒

87

Expectations

What do your parents, or others (grandparents, friends, teachers,) expect of you? Do you need to look a certain way? Do you have to be above average? Are you expected to excel at activities that someone else has chosen for you? Are you at all times expected to act as an adult? Or do you feel that there are too few expectations asked of you? Are other's expectations of you the same as your own? How realistic are they? Are they achievable, even if you wanted them?

Write your own version of the poem *You Wanted*, then later write how you integrate what they want with what you want in a poem entitled, *What I Want.*

BENEATH THE SICK-A-WAR TREE

Your sycamore branches, thick with hearted leaves,
don't cool a northerner in your smothering shade.

Beneath this canopy of southern hospitality
no grass grows, your heart allows only filtered light.

My child plays under your care, feels your burden
and names you, *Sick-A-War*. We are not safe here.

You hate my voice, my choices, my strange name,
in this forced-to-change plantation world.

I am haunted by swaying limbs, and bodies who swung there,
whose color was wrong or whose lips would not keep silent.

I tred softly on your prickly soil, aware of land mines,
fallen seed-balls, protecting your birthright with affliction.

89

 A Safe Place

Where do you feel safe? Where do you feel unsafe? Are you safe even if "your lips would not keep silent"? Where do you fit in? Do you feel as though you have to become someone else, say other people's words, or assume other people's values to fit in, to be accepted or to be loved? Do you feel as though you walk around on "prickly soil"? What "land mines" lie hidden? Whose "birthright" is being protected, with what kind of "affliction"? Are you "sick-a-war"?

Imagine a huge spreading oak (a safe tree) under which you sprawl. This is a place where you don't need to pretend. You are in control here. You are yourself here. You crawl up to a Y in the tree trunk and find a place to sit high above your world. You look around. You say, "I like that," and "I like that," and "I don't like that," and you say, "I'm okay. I have choices."

In this safe place write a poem called *High in the Safe Tree.*

CARRIED AWAY

I know I did wrong,
       got carried away
              like a storm-swollen stream,

my actions, full of stones,
       long pointed branches and
              thrown away debris.

The stream came from somewhere deep,
       a spring filled too full
              rising beyond its cistern.

You didn't need the finger in my face,
       the tight jaw, the snarling,
              as though I should remain forever

a dormant spring within a well,
       never clearing its dead debris
              nor cooling its outer edges,

never swelling high enough
       to flood our cozy home,
              to seep into its carpet.

Shame

Are you a bad person, or are you a person who sometimes does bad things, i.e. chooses behavior that results in unfavorable consequences? Do you know when you have made a mistake? How does it feel when someone shakes a finger in your face and says, "Shame on you" or "I told you so"? Are you able to learn from your own mistake, or do you need someone to point it out to you? What does the imposition of guilt and shame do for your ability to learn and/or change behavior? Is there a time limit on how long this behavior can be brought up against you, especially if there has been an apology and a change in behavior?

Write a rhyming poem about your feelings associated with guilt and shame, and your ability to overcome them. Call it *Can't Stand the Shame*.

CAN'T STAND THE SHAME

I can't stand the shame.

Am I forever to blame

-

-

-

-

SKIPPIN' TIME

One skip
Two skip
She's watchin'
Don't slip
Mother says
Can't call
Three skip
That's all
She says
Eat that meal
Four skip
What a deal!
Five skip
Six skip
She's still pushin'
What a trip
I say *leave*
Me alone
Mother says *don't*
Like that tone
Seven skip
TV's gone
Eight skip
Line's drawn
Mother's got
An eagle eye
Worse than
A Russian spy
I'm tired
Of this rhyme
Packed my bag
It's skippin' time

〜〜
〜〜

Relating to Parents and Significant Others

Have you ever wanted to run away from home? Do one, or both, of your parents watch you with an "eagle eye?" Does someone watch what you put on your plate, what you eat and don't eat, and watch with an accusing eye every time you head for the bathroom? Have they taken it on themselves to "cure" your eating problem? Have they taken away possessions or privileges? How does that feel to you? Is it working for you? In this poem a teen threatens to run away from home. Would that solve his/her problems?

Write your own jump-rope rhymes from both your own and your parent's (or counselor's) point of view.

One skip

Two skip

Feel like I

Wanna rip

-

-

-

-

-

-

ring of love beads

in '68 we let our hair grow long, dangled love
beads over peasant blouses thin enough
to spy both skin and shadow

we knew they didn't give peace a chance
hadn't loved anything but money,
didn't know our kind of love

the kind you cannot buy with commercial
smiles or money earned from their
military/industrial complex

dads threw us out while mothers cried
We tried our best, and sent cash
and letters signed *I love you*

it would never happen to our children, given
time and talk, books instead of guns,
not even sticks to aim

but they shave their heads, tattoo thigh
roses, hang rings from their noses
and use our language

to aim sharp words shot straight
as arrows into the target of our
ecological/wellness complex

they say, can't party on baked potato chips
can't get rich writing letters
or reading books

i send cash for therapy and leave messages
on e-mail *did best i could*
love you, mom

Trading Places

Have you ever thought what it must be like to be your parents, your friend, your spouse? Is there someone in your family who really is trying to relate to you, understand what you are going through? Do you feel loved by someone, even though he/she doesn't seem to understand you? Is there a way to communicate with that person? Have you tried? When you try to communicate what happens? Can you look that person in the eye and say, "I know you love me. But do you love me enough to really listen to me, to talk about the family secrets, and to talk about dysfunction in this family?"

Below, write down the issues you would talk about if they could be talked about in an honest, straight-forward fashion. Write it into a poem called *To Spy Both Skin and Shadow.*

IX.   INTERACTING

WITH THE WORLD

LEAVING BEHIND
(to a son leaving for college)

Middle of the night you wanted to be born.
Your brain stopped you.
Too big to descend,

doctors pulled you out and made you scream
and you continued for ten months of
cicada-screeching colic.

Never settled down, your brain stopped you
as you tried to descend
to games boys play,

to games parents play, games teachers play.
You changed rules, no pretending,
no forgetting, no lying,

no following of other's paths, no falling into line,
only the listening to the inner screech
of a lone cicada.

As you mount the airplane its high-pitched whirr
tells me you are where you should be.
Your battled brain will not

allow you to descend. You are climbing the limbs
of the tree leaving your brittle carcass
clawing at the lower bark.

Assertiveness

Do you know someone like the person described in the poem, someone who does everything his/her own way, one who can't be told anything by anyone? This type of aggressive person often gets what he/she wants through sheer force, but what are the consequences? How about the opposite? Do you know anyone who is passive and always follows every rule without complaint, never voicing his/her own thoughts or feelings about it? What are the consequences of each? What about a third alternative, called assertiveness?

An assertive person speaks up for himself/herself, but does it in a way that does not infringe on the feelings or the rights of others. Do you know how to talk to a person in authority and get your point across and/or your needs listened to? Think about this: Do you respond in a passive, aggressive or assertive way to your parents, your teachers, older peers, doctors, to people with ideas different from your own?

Decide which style is yours. Then write an acrostic poem about how it works for you or gets you into trouble. Choose the word "assertive," "aggressive" or "passive" and write it vertically on the page. Write a poem with each line beginning with the first letter of your chosen word.

-

-

-

-

-

-

-

-

-

HE LOVES ME

only the yellow

eye

remains
after ox-eye
daisy petals
are pulled
out

one

by

one

to envision
love

What Does Love Mean

What is your vision of love? Draw in daisy petals below, and then write characteristics of different kinds of love including parental love, romantic love, friendship, familial love in the petals. Do these characteristics of love work both for the other person and from the other person? Are they transient or permanent? Are they self-giving or self-sustaining? What does it mean to love pizza, to love learning, to love your dog? What is the relationship between loving others and loving yourself?

What is the relationship between loving your physical body and loving your mind or spirit?

Write a poem called *Gathering the Petals*.

now that he's gone

they say i'm strong
don't want to be strong

like an iron bar
don't want to be tough

like a green limb
i'm not young any more

like the scent of a skunk
please don't stay away

i want to flow like liquid chocolate into the mold of your soul

and wrap us in
crimson cellophane

the hollow inside
large enough for two

Grief

When we experience a loss it feels as though there is an emptiness inside us. Sometimes we reach for food to fill that emptiness, but it doesn't really address the problem. Sometimes food is the last thing we want and others have to remind us to eat and take care of ourselves.

How do you deal with grief and loss? Do you have a support system of friends and/or relatives to help you get through the rough times? Do you ever write about your feelings of loss?

Choose a loss in your life from the past or the present and write about it. Call it *The Hollow Inside.*

SECOND STORY

I've met all my neighbors except the man next door,
no moving day cookies, no advice on hardware stores,

he gets Friday lawn service, maid on Monday,
mail through a slot, and no delivered paper.

I watch his car leave the tombed garage early
and come home after all color of sun is gone,

darkened window glass hiding his face
like the skin of eggplant surrounding green flesh.

Facing my house, his second story window,
always dark and filled with shelves of cactus,

overlooks my old redbud tree, hole-filled,
barely hanging on for one last spring.

This morning as I lift my bedroom shade I see
its budlike flowers gliding along each branch

like water lilies outlining a beaver's trail. I feel
my neighbor's eyes, know he sees this one last show,

this sunrise burst of life in pink and green --
his gaze, a farewell to the only neighbor he knows.

♒

Support System

Do you have one? It's very difficult to make changes in your life without having supportive people around you. Who supports you in the healthy decisions you make?

Find people who will listen and take the time to be with you when needed. It's sad when our only support comes from nature. A beautiful tree or a sunset can inspire us or calm us, but we need people in our lives to support us.

Don't allow yourself to become as isolated as the man in the poem. Think about the people in your life. Do you support them, or do they support you? Or is it mutual? List the names of the people in your life. Then rank them in order of how much they support you. You know what support means, not being preachy or judgmental, but someone who listens and responds to your real needs.

Finally, write a poem called *Who's Helping Whom?*

PAISLEY DRESS OF PURPLE

When she told me to wear black, I said I would wear paisley,
dark and wiggling fabric draped over my tight shoulders,

this fabric massaging flesh and something else
deeply wounded in my thirteen year old frame.

I love the shapes of paisley as they whirl and
twist, colors blending into the last light of sunset,

the almost-dark time when shades of purple spread
across the sky, creep into air and take over my breath.

I chose the paisley dress for father's funeral,
it's dim light all that was left of day.

Dealing With Authority

Are you tired of taking orders? Unfortunately there will always be someone in authority over you. There are always laws, bosses, and people who have the authority to enforce their orders. Here is a good phrase to remember. "Do what they say, but do it your way." That's what the teen in the poem does. Instead of arguing about not wearing black to the funeral, she finds something dark to wear, something in a wiggling pattern (paisley.)

There is always wiggle room within any law or authoritative statement. This doesn't mean that you should try to manipulate those in authority. It means that you have some degree of freedom even when you have to follow orders. Think about one rule that you must follow. What is the wiggle room?

Write a poem with the title *Here in My Wiggle Room.*

PARK AND SHOP
After my son noticed that 'park and shop' backwards is 'pohs and krap'

      at the Park and Shop
you come to be seen. you come to pose in clothes
with the right labels and step inside to shelves of crap,
cigarettes, booze, stems of 75 cent satin roses with
cardboard heart and space to sign your name or your X.

      at the Park and Shop

iron bars protect windows with faded pictures
of half nude ladies and their johnny walker red
posing for cowboys in jeans tight enough to make
them sterile. here they sell rolls of lotto tickets,
used ones underfoot, all hope of winning gone.

      life's a gamble

for at night patron's designer label jackets
hide bullets and guns, no turn of the bin
for winners and losers, just a turn of the barrel
determines who gets trampled underfoot

      at the Park and Shop.

Violence

This Park and Shop is in a violent area of town. This poem talks not only about violence, but also about gambling. Do you have a choice about the violence in your life? Are your eating and/or your exercise habits causing violence toward your body. Is your life a gamble, a "turn of the bin for winners and losers"? Or do you have a choice? What is that choice? Are you getting "trampled underfoot"?

Do you believe that life is just a pose (pohs) and that everything in it is full of crap (krap)? Or can you Park and Shop elsewhere?

Spell your name backwards. What does it sound like or suggest to you? Title your poem by that name. Write your thoughts about freedom and fate, violence and peace.

X. HEALTH AND WELLNESS

SOMETHING STOLEN

Prisoners used to wear stripes (who cared if they defiled the zebra?)
but one too many must have run away blending in with nature's cover.

Jails now send out work crews in noxious jumpsuits of neon orange
not matched in nature except in Florida fruit and October maples.

I bought an orange wool coat, on sale. No one else wanted it.
Its wool will warm the coming winter, its brightness ward off the dark,

like the orange heather suit and soft sweater I wore the night we met,
bittersweet pinned in my cornsilk hair, lipstick to match autumn's brilliance.

Now I wrap the wool coat around me as I pick pyrocantha berries and hunt
orange mushrooms, remembering not prisoners, but something stolen.

Remembering Health

You had something bright and beautiful, and now it's gone? The above poem alludes to lost love. It doesn't tell us enough about what happened, only that it is now gone, stolen. What has been stolen from you, your childhood innocence, your health, the easiness of life?

Researchers are telling us that those who are chronically ill forget what health feels like. They need help remembering the feeling of being free of worry or pain, feeling whole and full of energy. The above poem was written around the color orange.

Choose a color that represents health and wholeness to you. Brainstorm several associations with that color, and then write a poem (Maybe write it in that color ink or crayon) which helps you recall something stolen from you, and now beginning to return.

TIMELESS

Summers seemed eternal
the year my lithe body
turned nine.

Solitaire and working
within the lines of
coloring books

took up time, but not easily,
so I wandered worn
paths of deer

and raccoon, thinking
they might lead
somewhere.

I found sprays of wild
black raspberries,
stayed all day,

picked amidst the thorns,
then traipsed home
with cheeks

and hands stained
from berries and
blood.

Summers now seem to
disappear as easily
as deer

in the city. Maybe I
should try solitaire
again,

make each day drag by
in waiting-in-line
time

or paint by number
someone else's
art.

Instead I follow paths
on yellow paper
pads

and find phrases of wild
description. I pick
and choose

words amidst confusion,
slowing time
enough

to write them into poems,
arriving home
with

tatooed fingers stained
from ink and
age.

〜〜
〜〜

Right Brain Activities

Does it seem as though there is never enough time, and yet there are times that drag by so slowly and never seem to move on? Is there any way that we can control time, or at least wrestle out a piece for ourselves? I have found that writing enables time to stop for me.

When I am writing poetry, or journaling, my body actually feels as though I am outside of the dimension of time. Scientists tell us that it has to do with alpha waves and the use of the right side of the brain. I just know that when I feel like yelling "Stop the world I want to get off," a pen and paper are my ticket to sanity. In my writing I can let go of all of my feelings, especially the ones no one else wants to hear. My journal never gives me that look which says *All right, I'll listen if I have to.*

What experiences do you enjoy so much that you forget time? Take time for those experiences that you value. Write about them. Give your writing the title *Slowing Time Enough to...*

TEST COMING UP

When an exam's coming
Heather starts chompin,'
but I can't swallow and
my legs start stompin'.
She finds the chips
and dips and cake
while I get a lump
in my throat and
an ache. She eats
all the cookies in the
kitchen and prowls
while I hold my stomach
as it starves and growls.
I don't know why when
I'm anxious or scared
food won't go down.
I know it's weird because
Heather keeps filling
her mouth with sweets,
(helps her concentrate
between the treats.)
We both get A's
on the exams we take,
after Heather purges
and my stomach aches.

Relaxation Techniques

What happens to you when you get nervous? Do you feel a lump in your throat or in your stomach? Do you lose your appetite . . . or maybe get even hungrier than normal? It's important to know the signs of anxiety. When you recognize them coming on you can then act to relax your body in a healthy manner using relaxation techniques such as: breathing deeply, walking slower, talking slower, singing a song, whistling, yawning, dancing, laughing . . . whatever it takes to get control of your anxiety.

Write a poem about something that makes you nervous and incorporate into that poem a healthy alternative behavior to address that anxiety. Call the poem *Untying the Nervous Knot.*

SONG OF A NORWEGIAN SUMMER DAY

A tow-headed boy pokes bushes for surprises,
digs to free a half-buried elk antler,
watches the scurrying of an upset anthill,
then picks berries not yet blue enough to eat.

He sings: la, la, loo, loo, loo, I am here
on this cold day of all-day-sun
the only one who remembers to have fun.
It is July. It is summer.

Gala Lake is clear as a window pane
outlined in gray granite, framed
with green mountain fir, and so cold
the bottom rocks themselves seem to shake.

Grandma eats reindeer sausage as she watches.
Grandpa's mittened fingers fish from shore.
Father shouts for the boy to hush, so he listens
for a moment to the wind and shaking rocks,

then sings: la, la, loo, loo, loo, I am here
on this cold day of all-day sun.
He pulls off socks, digs toes in wet sand
and lifts the antlers up into his white, tossled hair.

Mindfulness

The subject of this poem was a little boy on vacation in Norway. Everyone else around him thought that vacation was just an extension of work. But this little boy loved and cherished every moment, was excited by each tiny discovery, and was not affected by sour faces and negative attitudes of the adults around him. He sang from pure joy. He was "in the moment." That is the definition of mindfulness. If the berry that this child picked was too green, he didn't care, because the joy of discovery was good enough. Judging from the puckered look on his face, and then the giggle, he fully understood the concept of sour. He felt the cold air, the wet sand, tasted the sour blueberry, saw the crooked and bleached elk antlers, heard the wind, smelled the reindeer sausage. This child was living life fully. The sad part about it was that his father and grandparents were trying to discourage it. How can you be mindful of how your body feels and how your food tastes so that you can be truly satisfied?

Take a juice-orange and cut it in half around the middle. Take one of the halves and squeeze its juice into your mouth. Can you feel your hand muscles working, your mouth and jaw moving into the correct position to collect the juice? How cold is the juice on your tongue? Is it sweet or sour? Does it taste better on the tip of your tongue or elsewhere in your mouth? Hold the juice in your mouth for a while before swallowing.

Do you still taste it as you swallow? Can you feel it moving down your esophagus, into your stomach?

Take a deep breath. Write about this experience.

SNOWY MORNING IN OKLAHOMA

Like white chocolate on mixed nuts
the snow coats this crazy world
and makes it sweet.

I open my morning shade, spy
the sparse white snow.
My body sighs.

It is an old feeling, from cold
northern winters, when this
blanket of white

reflected the half light of a
low lying sun, and told my
eyes to blink.

On mornings of white I do not
think. I allow my breath
to slow.

This snow, this breath, this
moment. I blink, I sigh,
I know.

Meditation

Meditation is a way of slowing the mind, centering the consciousness on a peaceful phrase or object. Morning snow in Oklahoma does that for my brain. But meditation can also occur through the use of deep breathing. What does this have to do with a healthy lifestyle? Doctors tell us that it can relieve stress and tension. Psychologists tell us it helps to quiet our lives and allows us to concentrate on what is important.

Slowly breathe in to the count of five, then let go to the count of five. Continue this slow, deep breathing. If your brain starts telling you about the activities of the day, or questioning you as to the value of this meditation, then push those thoughts out of your consciousness by repeating the word, "Peace" or "Calm." It is important to be in a quiet place, with no distractions. You may want to light a fragrant candle. It may also help to imagine a peaceful place, a seashore, a mountain top, a rocking chair. Practice meditating for one minute, the next day two minutes, and continue until you feel comfortable with this practice. Take time daily for meditation.

On this page write about your peaceful place, so that you may visualize it easily when you begin your deep breathing and meditation. What does it look like, smell like, feel like? What do you hear? Are you alone there or is someone with you? What colors are present? How does it make you feel? Give your writing the title *My Refuge of Peace.*

REBEL

You entered my therapy office,
the fourth in three years.

"You're seventeen and worse than a rebel –
more like a devil," says your mom.

They've taken away your car, your phone,
your freedom, nothing's worked – now they've

taken your dresser, your mirror, your bed, the door.
Your mattress lies on the floor stripped

of crisp sheets and fluffy pillows,
no privacy until you behave.

You know exactly what you want and
with every taking you become more the rebel.

I say STOP! Where are you in this taking
away of things, this taking away of you?

You are in the poem. You have been
given paper, you have been given

back the pen. You have recovered
your voice, your spirit. You

are flowing into the words,
flowing into recovery.

Poetry Therapy

Has writing given you a voice? Has writing given you a way not only to express your feelings, but also a way to engage them?

Allow poetry to say the things you never dared to say. Allow poetry to touch the parts of your heart you thought were numb. Allow the reading of poetry to send your imagination into areas never dreamed of. Allow poetry to soothe you, to rescue you, to be your non-judgmental friend. A Simon and Garfunkel song says, "I have my poetry to protect me."

Write a poem about how you are using poetry to heal. Call your poem *I Have My Poetry to Protect Me.*

About the Author

Cynthia Gustavson was born in rural Minnesota to a jazz musician and a waitress in 1947. She is the author of five poetry collections, several poetry therapy workbooks, and has been published in numerous journals. She was educated at Gustavus Adolphus College, Boston University, Louisiana State University, United Seminary of the Twin Cities, and Oklahoma State University, has taught at Northeastern State University in Tallequah, Oklahoma, and Louisiana State University in Shreveport, Louisiana, and has been an invited lecturer around the country.

In her twenty-three years as a social worker she has worked in drug prevention, practiced individual and group therapy, worked extensively with caregivers of the chronically ill and developmentally disabled.

Winner of a New Millennium Writings Award in 2002 and finalist for the Rita Dove Poetry Award from the Salem College Center for Women Writers in 2004, Gustavson lives and works in Tulsa, Oklahoma with her husband of 37 years.

More information can be found at www.cynthiagustavson.com